Discover and
Explore the
Everyday World
With Your Child

Let's Go to the Market!

Barbara Dullaghan, M.Ed.,
Nancy B. Hertzog, Ph.D.,
& Ellen Honeck, Ph.D.

Prufrock Press Inc.
Waco, Texas

Prufrock Press Inc., P.O. Box 8813, Waco, TX 76714-8813
Phone: (800) 998-2208 ● http://www.prufrock.com

The Smart Start Series

To Caregivers: Let's Go to the Market!

How to Enjoy This Book With Your Child

Early literacy development begins with spoken language. The more your child talks, the more vocabulary words your child will learn. You will enjoy talking to your child when discussing his or her own ideas! This book promotes early literacy by engaging you and your child in conversation about the book's photographs.

We encourage you to ask three types of open-ended thinking questions:

- **Creative:** Creative questions focus on developing original solutions, products, or processes.

- **Critical:** Critical questions emphasize a dynamic process of questioning and reasoning; may include evaluation of known ideas to produce new ideas.

- **Mathematical:** Mathematical questions engage children in thinking numerically and in patterns; they allow for problem solving, conjectures, and generalizations.

We also encourage you to document or write down your child's responses, read the book again, and see if your child has new and more elaborate ideas. Create a space in your house where you and your child can display the responses to the photographs and revisit them. Elaborating upon or modifying original ideas strengthens your child's disposition to seek alternative responses and to continue to engage in learning.

We hope this book provides you with many ideas for developing your own open-ended questions to engage your child in higher levels of thinking. We would love to hear some of your child's creative ideas about these photographs. Visit the book's webpage at http://www.prufrock.com/Assets/ClientPages/SmartStart.aspx to get more ideas for extending your child's thinking.

Finally, we hope you enjoy the time spent in conversation with your child!

People all around the world go to markets
to get their food. Have you ever been
to an indoor or outdoor market?

Creative Thinking

What could we make with the
vegetables in this photograph?

Critical Thinking

How do you decide which ones to buy?

Mathematical Thinking

What are the different shapes
you see in the photograph?

Have you ever been shopping with your mother or father? Let's talk about the shopping trip in the picture.

Creative Thinking

What might be on the man's shopping list?

Critical Thinking

How are the vegetables on the shelves organized?

Mathematical Thinking

How much do you think these vegetables weigh: carrots, corn, lettuce, and squash?

People eat different types of bread all over the world. This photograph shows a variety of breads.

Creative Thinking

Create a story in which you are a type of bread (for example, baguette, ciabatta, Challah, pita, focaccia).

Critical Thinking

How are the breads in the picture alike and different?

Mathematical Thinking

What do you think determines the shape and size of bread?

The boy is at a fish market. Let's talk about a fish market.

Creative Thinking
Can you tell a story about what the boy might be thinking?

Critical Thinking
How did the fish get to the market?

Mathematical Thinking
How many of these fish would we need to make a fish stew? How could we figure that out?

This girl is looking at plums.
Let's talk about the fruit stand.

Creative Thinking
What fruits could you add to the ones in
the photograph to make a fruit salad?

Critical Thinking
How will the girl select the right
plum without tasting it first?

Mathematical Thinking
Estimate how many plums
are on the table.

These girls are looking into a bakery case. If you could select a dessert, what would you choose?

Creative Thinking
What are all the toppings you could put on a cupcake?

Critical Thinking
If you were these girls, how would you decide what to buy?

Mathematical Thinking
What patterns do you see in this photograph?

Extension Questions

Selecting Vegetables

- How are the vegetables sorted?
- How many cucumbers would you need to buy to make a salad for your family?
- What do you think the cucumber feels like?

Shopping With Dad

- What are some foods you might put on a shopping list?
- What food would Dad want to put in the cart? What food do you want to put in the cart?
- How do you think vegetables stay fresh at the supermarket?

Choosing Bread

- What kind of bread would you choose to make your favorite sandwich?
- What are some ingredients in bread?
- Explain why some bread is flatter than other types of bread.

Buying Fish at the Market

- Can you tell a story about why the boy is looking so intently at the bowl of fish?
- What are some different types of fish that we eat?
- How many ways can you buy fish (for example, in a can or from a tank)?

Picking Just the Right One

- There are many fruits on this table. How do you think they got there?
- Do the different colors reflect the taste of the fruit?
- Have you ever tasted a kiwi or a kumquat?

Looking for Dessert

- If 12 cupcakes cost $12, how much does one cupcake cost?
- Tell a story about why the girls are buying cupcakes.
- Can you estimate how many cupcakes the bakery sells everyday?

For more great ideas, visit our webpage at www.prufrock.com/Assets/ClientPages/SmartStart.aspx